PUFFIN BOOKS

FANTASTIC Mr Fox
A PLAY

Roald Dahl was born in 1916 in Wales of Norwegian parents. He was educated in England before starting work for the Shell Oil Company in Africa. He began writing after a 'monumental bash on the head' sustained as an RAF fighter pilot during the Second World War. Roald Dahl is one of the most successful and well known of all children's writers. His books, which are read by children the world over, include *James and the Giant Peach, Charlie and the Chocolate Factory, The Magic Finger, Charlie and the Great Glass Elevator, Fantastic Mr Fox, Matilda, The Twits, The BFG, The Witches*, winner of the 1983 Whitbread Award, and *Danny the Champion of the World*. Roald Dahl died in 1990 at the age of seventy-four.

D1103087

ROALD DAHL

FANTASTIC Mr Fox

A PLAY

ADAPTED BY SALLY REID
INTRODUCTION BY ROALD DAHL

PUFFIN

Find out more about Roald Dahl and the adapted plays
by visiting the website roalddahl.com

PERFORMANCE RIGHTS:
All rights whatsoever in this play are strictly reserved, and application for performance, etc.,
should be made before rehearsals commence to: Casarotto Ramsay & Associates Ltd, Waverley House,
7–12 Noel Street, London WIF 8GQ.

No performances may be given unless a licence has been obtained.
The publication of this play does not necessarily indicate its availability for performance.

PUFFIN BOOKS

Published by the Penguin Group
Penguin Books Ltd, 80 Strand, London WC2R ORL, England
Penguin Group (USA) Inc., 375 Hudson Street, New York, New York 10014, USA
Penguin Group (Canada), 90 Eglinton Avenue East, Suite 700, Toronto, Ontario, Canada M4P 2Y3
(a division of Pearson Penguin Canada Inc.)
Penguin Ireland, 25 St Stephen's Green, Dublin 2, Ireland (a division of Penguin Books Ltd)
Penguin Group (Australia), 707 Collins Street, Melbourne, Victoria 3008, Australia
(a division of Pearson Australia Group Pty Ltd)
Penguin Books India Pvt Ltd, 11 Community Centre, Panchsheel Park, New Delhi – 110 017, India
Penguin Group (NZ), 67 Apollo Drive, Rosedale, Auckland 0632, New Zealand
(a division of Pearson New Zealand Ltd)
Penguin Books (South Africa) (Pty) Ltd, Block D, Rosebank Office Park, 181 Jan Smuts Avenue, Parktown North,
Gauteng 2193, South Africa

Penguin Books Ltd, Registered Offices: 80 Strand, London WC2R ORL, England

puffinbooks.com

First published simultaneously by Unwin Hyman and Puffin Books 1987
Reissued 2001 and 2014
001

Text and illustrations copyright © Roald Dahl Nominee Ltd and Sally Reid, 1987
Title-page illustrations copyright © Quentin Blake, 2014
All rights reserved

The moral right of the author and illustrators has been asserted

Set in Monophoto Baskerville
Printed in Great Britain by Clays Ltd, St Ives plc

Except in the United States of America, this book is sold subject to the condition that it shall not,
by way of trade or otherwise, be lent, re-sold, hired out, or otherwise circulated without the publisher's
prior consent in any form of binding or cover other than that in which it is published and without
a similar condition including this condition being imposed on the subsequent purchaser

British Library Cataloguing in Publication Data
A CIP catalogue record for this book is available from the British Library

ISBN: 978-0-141-37696-7

www.greenpenguin.co.uk

Penguin Books is committed to a sustainable
future for our business, our readers and our planet.
This book is made from Forest Stewardship
Council™ certified paper.

CONTENTS

This dramatic adaptation of *Fantastic Mr Fox* was first presented in the Easter Term 1987 by the children and staff of St Andrew's C.E. Primary School, Buckland Monachorum, Devon.

INTRODUCTION

Back in 1976, a school-teacher in America called Richard George sent me his own dramatized version of *Charlie and the Chocolate Factory*. Everyone over here liked it and Puffin were happy to publish it as a guide to other teachers who wanted to put on a school play of this book. Mr George subsequently dramatized and had published two of my other books, *Charlie and the Great Glass Elevator* and *James and the Giant Peach*.

Plenty of other school-teachers in many parts of the world have sent me their own dramatized versions of one or another of my books, but not until Mrs Sally Reid from Buckland Monachorum in Devon sent me her adaptation of *Fantastic Mr Fox* did I think that any of them was really good enough to send on to the publisher.

Mrs Reid's manuscript arrived at my house in December 1985, and it was accompanied by a letter that was notable for its modesty. She said, 'Throughout the ten years or so of reading your stories to my children, my favourite has always been *Fantastic Mr Fox* . . . I have always wanted to see it performed as a play and I have taken the liberty of writing a script . . . I do hope you enjoy reading it as much as I have enjoyed writing it. I enclose an s.a.e. for the return of the script.'

I did enjoy reading it and I wrote back to Mrs Reid,

telling her that I had sent her work on to Puffin for their consideration. She replied, saying, 'Thank you so much for your letter. It is the most exciting one I have ever had . . .'

On Christmas Eve 1985, a note came from Elizabeth Attenborough at Puffin, saying that they would publish. I immediately picked up the phone and called Mrs Reid in Devonshire with the news. It is always an enormous pleasure to be able to give someone good tidings like this, especially at Christmas. Sally Reid wrote to me again after that, saying, '. . . my children now fight each other to the phone whenever it rings in case it's Roald Dahl on the line again . . .'

Apart from all that, this play is very skilfully adapted from the book, and I believe it will be welcomed by teachers and children everywhere who wish to put on a school play that is neither too long nor too complicated. It should be a lot of fun to do.

ROALD DAHL

FANTASTIC MR FOX

CAST OF CHARACTERS

(In order of appearance)

Farmer Boggis
Farmer Bunce
Farmer Bean
First Child
Second Child
Third Child
Other Children
Small Fox 1
Small Fox 2
Small Fox 3
Small Fox 4
Mrs Fox
Mr Fox
Badger
Small Badger

Rat
The Voice of Mrs Bean
Mabel
Mrs Badger
Three Small Badgers
Mole
Mrs Mole
Four Small Moles
Rabbit
Mrs Rabbit
Five Small Rabbits
Weasel
Mrs Weasel
Six Small Weasels

SYNOPSIS OF SCENES

SCENE I

BOGGIS, BUNCE *and* BEAN *are seated at three tables placed in a line on stage in front of the drawn curtains. They are 'frozen'. The tables are laden with the appropriate food and drink, i.e., chicken, doughnuts and flagons of cider. Lights are off at this point. Children enter from back of hall* [*spotlight*]. *They skip, run and laugh up the centre aisle, chanting*:

CHILDREN: Boggis and Bunce and Bean,
　　　　　　One fat, one short, one lean,
　　　　　　These horrible crooks,
　　　　　　So different in looks,
　　　　　　Were none the less equally mean.
　　　　　[*Children sit on steps at front of stage. As each farmer is mentioned, a spotlight pans on to him and he becomes alive, eating or drinking revoltingly*]

FIRST CHILD: Let's sit down a minute.

SECOND CHILD: What shall we do? We could go up to the woods and play.

THIRD CHILD: Or we could go down to the river.

FIRST CHILD: Better not. My mum says I'm not to go anywhere near the valley 'cos of those three nasty men. You know the ones – they're always talking together in low whispers and looking over their shoulders to see if anyone's listening. The dreaded Boggis, Bunce and Bean, no less.

SECOND CHILD: My mum says the same. She says not only are they the nastiest farmers in the whole county, they're also the richest. They never spend any money and they pay miserable wages to everyone who works for them. They store all the money they get from selling their chickens and ducks and geese in great padlocked chests.

THIRD CHILD: Which do you think is the worst?

SECOND CHILD: Don't know. They've all got such horrible habits. [*Laughter*]

FIRST CHILD: I think old Boggis is the worst. [*Spotlight on* BOGGIS] He's got absolutely thousands of chickens locked away in those chicken houses. And he's so *fat*. He's got a head like the top of a boiled egg and a bristly, greasy moustache. D'you know, he eats three boiled chickens smothered with dumplings every day for breakfast, lunch and supper? I can just see him eating the chicken legs in his fingers and all the grease getting in his moustache and running down his chin.

CHILDREN: Ugh!

SECOND CHILD: What about that pot-bellied dwarf Bunce then? [*Spotlight on* BUNCE] He keeps thousands of ducks and geese. He lives on doughnuts and goose livers. He mashes the livers into a disgusting paste and then stuffs the paste into the doughnuts.

It gives him such a tummy ache he's always in a foul temper. You should see his kitchen – it's filthy, and the stench hits you even before you open the door.

THIRD CHILD: Ah, but I don't believe there can be anyone more disgusting or revolting than old Bean. [*Spotlight on* BEAN] He's the one that keeps those thousands of turkeys in that orchard full of apples. He's as thin as Boggis is fat – but what's more, he's clever, cleverest of them all. He doesn't eat any food at all, just drinks gallons of strong cider made from all those apples. And he never washes. His earholes are clogged with all kinds of muck and wax and bits of chewing gum and dead flies . . .

CHILDREN: Stop! Ugh! [*Laughing*] No more!

FIRST CHILD: Anyway, I reckon we'd better not go anywhere near their place today. Mum says she saw them in town yesterday. Furious they were, cursing and swearing. There's some sly fox that keeps sneaking up in the night and taking all their chickens and ducks and things.

SECOND CHILD: And can't they catch him? I bet they're hopping mad.

THIRD CHILD: Seems not. They keep trying to, of course, but it's a clever old fox. Outwits them night after night.

SECOND CHILD: Good luck to him, I say, serves them right for being so disgusting. [*Laughs*]
   [*Exit down aisle chanting and chattering as lights come up on stage*]

BOGGIS [*Banging fists on table*]: Dang and blast that lousy beast!

BUNCE: I'd like to rip his guts out!

BEAN [*Sinister*]: He must be killed.

BOGGIS: Hundreds of chickens have I lost to that sly fox. Night after night I've gone out after him with my gun, and night after night has he given me the slip. But I'll get him, and when I do he'll be in that pot, stewing along with the dumplings. Fox stew, that's what I'll be having. Ha ha!

BUNCE: Not if I get my hands on him first he won't. I'll be cooking his liver and mashing it up to put in my doughnuts. He'll not be eating many more of my ducks, I'll be telling you. I'll catch him one day – you mark my words, I've got to catch him.

BEAN [*Coolly*]: All I want to see is his rotten carcass hanging up in my cellar. Strung up [*Savouring the picture*] so he can never sneak in and take one of my plump turkeys ever again. He's outwitted us for too long now. He's made absolute fools of us. Every time we get near him, he heads off in the other direction. It's almost as if he smells us on the wind.

BUNCE: Us? How could he smell us? I wash every Friday.

BEAN [*Moving to front of tables, centre stage*]: He must be killed.

BOGGIS [*Moving beside* BEAN]: But how? How on earth can we catch the blighter?
[BUNCE *moves to join them*]

BEAN: I have a plan . . .

BUNCE: You've never had a decent plan yet.

BEAN: Shut up and listen. Things are a little different now. I have been thinking – an activity unknown to either of you two. Tomorrow night we will all hide just outside the hole where the fox lives. We will be silent. We will be patient. And what is more, we will choose our positions *very* carefully. We will make sure that the wind is not blowing from us towards the fox's hole. That way we shall not be 'smelled out'. We will wait there until he comes out then . . . BANG, BANG, BANG!

BUNCE: Very clever, *very* intelligent. Just one thing, first we have to find the hole.

BEAN: That, my dear Bunce, is exactly why I said things were a little different. I have already found it.

It's up in the wood on the hill. Hidden, oh, so carefully hidden, under a huge tree ... [*Turning to face
audience*] And there, Mr Fox, we will be meeting
with you tonight.

    [*Lights out.* BOGGIS, BUNCE and BEAN *exit
through curtains*]

End of Scene 1

SCENE 2

Curtains open, revealing most of the stage taken up with the inside of the FOXES' *hole. Stage left is a door with steps leading out to a steep bank on top of which stands a large tree.* SMALL FOXES *are engaged in playing a board game.* MRS FOX *is ironing.*

SMALL FOX 1: Your turn, come on.

SMALL FOX 2: Six. I move six places. One, two, three, four, five, six. [*All peer at board*] Hooray! I'm winning.

SMALL FOX 1: Only just. I was winning first, don't forget. Besides, I let you off when I landed on you last time.

SMALL FOX 3: My turn. [*Throws dice and loses it. All scrabble about after it*] [*To* SMALL FOX 1] Bother! It's under your paw.

SMALL FOX 1: You're hopeless! You've already lost one dice.

SMALL FOX 3: Well, you shouldn't have your paws in the way. You always seem to have more paws than four paws.

[SMALL FOX 1 *stands up and looks on floor*]

SMALL FOX 4: There it goes! It's rolled into the corner. Look!

SMALL FOX 2 [*Plaintively*]: Oh no! I've never been winning before – and now you've lost the dice!

SMALL FOX 3 [*Looking in corner stage right*]: I can't find it! Someone help me!
　　[*General mêlée of fox brushes and paws*]

SMALL FOX 4: Maybe we should play something else.

MRS FOX [*Looking up*]: Now children, what *are* you doing? It's nearly your bedtime. One of you go and fetch your father's scarf – it's hanging on its peg. Hurry up now. [SMALL FOX 1 *goes out stage right to fetch it*] He's almost ready.

SMALL FOX 2 [*All thoughts of the game forgotten*]: Mum, how soon do you think we'll be able to go out with Dad on his expeditions?

SMALL FOX 3: Do you think it will be soon, Mum? I'd love to see the inside of Boggis's chicken house.

SMALL FOX 4: *So* would I.
MRS FOX: I don't know, dears. It'll be a long time before you're as clever and as cunning as your father. Now pack away your game.
　　[SMALL FOXES 2, 3 *and* 4 *do so.* MR FOX *enters right followed by* SMALL FOX 1, *carrying scarf. He goes over to a mirror on the wall, takes the scarf and adjusts it, with some finesse*]

MR FOX: Well, my darling, what shall it be tonight? A fine moonlight night like tonight. What shall I bring back for my beautiful wife?

MRS FOX [*Pondering*]: I think we'll have duck tonight. Bring us two fat ducks if you please. One for you and me, and one for the children.

MR FOX [*Smoothing his whiskers*]: Ducks it shall be! Bunce's best. That should make Bunce bounce with rage.

MRS FOX: Now do be careful.

MR FOX [*Comes over and puts his arm around her*]: My darling, I can smell those goons a mile away. You should know that. I can even smell one from the other. Boggis gives off a filthy stink of rotten chicken-skins. Bunce reeks of goose-livers, and as for Bean, the fumes of apple cider hang around him like poisonous gases. I don't intend that they shall ever catch me.
    [SMALL FOXES *laugh. He goes over and kisses each one in turn*]

SMALL FOX 1: Bye, Dad, wish I was coming with you.

MR FOX: And so you shall, one day.

SMALL FOX 2: When, Dad, will it be soon?

MR FOX: Soon enough.

SMALL FOX 3: They'll never ever catch you, will they Dad?

MR FOX: Not if I smell them first they won't.

SMALL FOX 4: I'm going to grow up just as clever as you, Dad.

MRS FOX [*As she kisses her husband goodbye*]: Now please, don't you get careless. You know they'll be waiting for you, all three of them.

MR FOX: Don't you worry about me. I shall go, oh, so very silently. Only the moon shall see me. And I shall be back very soon. Now you four be good. I'll see you later
[*Exits through door. Lights go out. Spotlight on* MR FOX. *Silence.* MR FOX *carefully climbs up steps. Cautiously looks out over top. Sniffs. Moves forward very slightly. Sniffs again. Edges out to waist. Sniffs. Hears rustle, freezes. Waits. Edges out almost completely. Long careful look round. BANG, BANG, BANG. He disappears immediately down through door*]

[*Spotlight on* BOGGIS, BUNCE *and* BEAN *who appear from behind tree and look down towards the* FOXES' *hole.*]

BEAN: Did we get him? [BOGGIS *shines torch on hole.* BEAN *stoops down and holds up tail*] We got the tail, but we missed the fox.
[*Tosses tail away*]

BOGGIS: Dang and blast! We shot too late. We should have let fly the moment he poked his head out.

BUNCE: He won't be poking it out again in a hurry.

BEAN [*Taking a swig from his flask*]: It'll take three days at least before he gets hungry enough to come out again. I'm not sitting here waiting for that. Let's dig him out.

BOGGIS: Ah! Now you're talking sense. We can dig him out in a couple of hours. We know he's there.

BUNCE: I reckon there's a whole family of them down that hole.

BEAN: Then we'll have the lot. Get the shovels!

End of Scene 2

SCENE 3

Inside FOXES' *hole.* MR FOX *is crouched bottom-up on the bed.* MRS FOX *is bandaging his stump.* SMALL FOXES *stand around with hot water, scissors, bandages, etc.*

MRS FOX: It was the finest tail for miles around.

MR FOX: It hurts!

MRS FOX: I know it does, sweetheart. But it'll soon get better.

SMALL FOX 1: And it will soon grow again, Dad.

MR FOX: It will never grow again. I shall be tail-less for the rest of my life. And to think that I let those goons do this to me. What was I thinking of? There was something in the air. There was just that little indefinable something in the air that wasn't right. I should have checked which way the wind was blowing. I should have known!

SMALL FOX 2: Gosh, Dad, just think if they'd shot a second earlier!

SMALL FOX 3: You must have been very quick.

SMALL FOX 4: Shooting at my father, indeed!
[*Reliving the scene*]

SMALL FOX 2: Everyone will know how you lost it, Dad, and think how brave you are!

MRS FOX: Hmm. [*Doubtfully*] Well, I've done my best. We must give it time to heal now. Come on, children, time to go to bed. [SMALL FOXES *curl up on large mat on floor*] And you, my darling, must get some sleep too. We'll think about it all in the morning. [*Turns out light*] Good-night.
[*Climbs into bed beside* MR FOX]

SMALL FOX 1: Good-night, Mum.

SMALL FOX 3: You're taking up all the room again. Good-night.

SMALL FOX 2: Good-night. Hey, wait a minute. What's this? [*Sits up*] I think I've found the dice!

SMALL FOX 1: Go to sleep.

SMALL FOX 4 [*Muttering*]: Shooting *my Dad*! Indeed! 'Night Mum. 'Night Dad.

MR FOX: Good-night, my dears. Ouch!
[*Silence as all sleep.* BOGGIS, BUNCE *and* BEAN, *carrying torches and shovels, enter stage left and begin shovelling noisily outside the* FOXES' *hole*]

MR FOX [*Sitting up suddenly*]: Wake up! Wake up! They're digging us out.

MRS FOX [*Whispering*]: Are you sure that's it?

MR FOX: I'm positive. Listen! [*All listen*] They're not going to give up. I might have known.

MRS FOX: They'll kill my children.

MR FOX: Never! [*Leaps out of bed*]

MRS FOX: But darling, they will! You know they will.

SMALL FOX 1: How will they kill us, Mummy?

SMALL FOX 2: Will there be dogs?

SMALL FOX 3: It won't be just our tails this time, will it?

SMALL FOX 4 [*Fists up*]: I'm ready for them.

SMALL FOX 2: Don't be silly, we'd never stand a chance.

SMALL FOX 3: They really mean it this time.

SMALL FOX 1 [*Wailing*]: What are we going to do?

MRS FOX: It's all right, my dears. Your father will think of something to outwit those awful men.
[*Loud scrunch. Door begins to split*]

MR FOX [*Suddenly aroused from deep thought*]: I've got it. Come on! There's not a moment to lose. Why didn't I think of it before?

SMALL FOX 4: Think of what, Dad?

SMALL FOX 1: Tell us quickly, Dad.

MR FOX: We dig. A fox can dig quicker than a man. Nobody in the world can dig as quick as a fox. Come on. Let's go.

[*Begins digging stage right*]

MRS FOX: Go downwards, Father says, children. Two of you clear the earth away as the rest of us dig.

MR FOX: Go downwards. That's it. We've got to go downwards. As deep as we possibly can. We'll beat their shovels. Come on. DIG.

[*Reach edge of stage right. Begin to head downwards, down ramp towards auditorium*]

SMALL FOX 1: My paws are aching!

SMALL FOX 2: Mine too.

SMALL FOX 3: We must keep going.

SMALL FOX 4 [*Muttering and digging furiously*]: We'll show 'em. We'll show 'em who can dig the fastest.

MRS FOX: Keep going, my dears. We'll soon be safe – follow your father's stump.

SMALL FOX 2 [*Pausing*]: The scrunching doesn't sound so loud.

SMALL FOX 1: No. It's definitely fainter.

SMALL FOX 3: Oh! I do hope we've lost them.

SMALL FOX 4 [*Still digging furiously*]: Dig us out indeed!

MR FOX [*Holding up his hand at bottom of ramp*]: Hold it!

[*Listening*] Phew! I think we've done it. They'll never get as deep as this. Well done, everyone!

SMALL FOXES: Phew!
[*All sit down, panting*]

MRS FOX [*To* SMALL FOXES]: I should like you to know that if it wasn't for your father we should all be dead by now. Your father is a fantastic fox.
[MR FOX *smiles at* MRS FOX. *There is a sudden crash as* BOGGIS, BUNCE *and* BEAN *break through the door.* FOXES *huddle in fright.* BOGGIS, BUNCE *and* BEAN, *seeing no foxes, move over to stage right at top of ramp*]

BOGGIS [*Kneeling with torch as if looking down tunnel*]: Dang and blast. He's not here. He's gone deeper. Whose rotten idea was this?

BUNCE: Bean's idea.
[BOGGIS *and* BUNCE *stare at* BEAN, *who takes another swig of cider and puts the flask back in his pocket*]

BEAN [*Angry*]: Listen. I want that fox. I'm going to get that fox. I'm not giving in 'til I've strung him up over my front porch, dead as a dumpling!

BOGGIS: We can't get him by digging, that's for sure. I've had enough of digging.

BUNCE [*To* BEAN]: Have you got any more stupid ideas, then?

BEAN: What? I can't hear you. [*Digging wax out of his ear*] Speak louder.

BUNCE [*Shouting*]: GOT ANY MORE STUPID IDEAS?

BEAN: What we need on this job are machines ... *mechanical* shovels. We'll have him out in five minutes with *mechanical* shovels!

BOGGIS *and* BUNCE: Mechanical shovels!

BEAN: All right then, Boggis, you stay here and see the fox doesn't escape. Bunce and I will go and fetch our machinery. If he tries to get out, shoot him quick.
[BEAN *and* BUNCE *exit left.* BOGGIS *trains his gun at the tunnel*]

End of Scene 3

SCENE 4

Sound of approaching mechanical shovels, falling trees, etc.
BUNCE *and* BEAN *enter stage left 'driving' large cardboard diggers.*

BOGGIS: Wonderful! Wonderful! Now we'll get him, the blighter.

BEAN: Here we go, then!

BUNCE: Death to the fox!
[*They start to dig away, with forward and backward movements, at the top of the ramp.* FOXES *are huddled together at the bottom of the ramp*]

SMALL FOX 1: What's happening, Dad?

SMALL FOX 2: What are they doing?

SMALL FOX 3: Dad, whatever is that noise?

MRS FOX: It's an earthquake!

SMALL FOX 4: Look! Our tunnel's got shorter!

SMALL FOX 2: I can see daylight!
[MR FOX *edges up ramp to investigate. Returns*]

MR FOX: Tractors! And *mechanical* shovels! Dig for your lives! Dig! Dig! Dig!

[*There ensues an underground chase, the directions of which can vary according to size and layout of the auditorium. Appropriate music may be played during periods of digging.* FOXES, *bent double, dig with front paws. They stop to listen at certain positions along the way (see staging plan on p. 75).* BOGGIS, BUNCE *and* BEAN *are always a set distance behind*]

MR FOX [*Position A*]: We're going to make it! I'm sure we are!

MRS FOX: I hope you're right, my darling. I just hope you're right.

SMALL FOX 1: Oh Dad, my paws are tired.

SMALL FOX 3: And mine are bleeding, look!

MRS FOX: Be brave. We must shake them off soon, surely.
   [*Loud crunching sound*]

MR FOX: Keep going, my darlings! Don't give up!
   [FOXES *start digging again down the aisle to Position B, and then, without stopping, out of auditorium doors at rear.* BOGGIS, BUNCE *and* BEAN *now reach Position A and stop digging.* BOGGIS *is in front, holds up torch and peers forward*]

BOGGIS: Keep going! [*Echoing* MR FOX] We'll get him any moment now!

BEAN: Have you caught sight of him yet?

BOGGIS: Not yet. But I think you're close!

BUNCE: I'll pick him up with my bucket! I'll chop him
to pieces! Hey there, Mr Fox! We're coming to get
you now!

BOGGIS: You've had your last chicken! You'll never
come prowling around *my* farm again! Faster! Faster!
[*Continue digging to Position B. Stop, exhausted.*
BUNCE *and* BEAN *get out of diggers*]

BOGGIS: Dang and blast that filthy stinking fox! [*Takes
out watch*] It's six o'clock and getting dark. What the
heck do we do now?

BEAN: I'll tell you what we *don't* do. We don't let him go!

BUNCE: We'll never let him go!

BOGGIS: Never, never, never!

BEAN [*Calling menacingly up tunnel, i.e. centre aisle in front
of him*]: Did you hear that, Mr Fox! – It's not over
yet, Mr Fox! We're not going home till we've strung
you up dead as a dingbat!

BUNCE: What's the next move?

BEAN: We're sending you down the hole to fetch him
up! Down you go, you miserable midget!

BUNCE [*Screams and backs away*]: Not me!

BEAN: Then there's only one thing to do. We starve
him out. We camp here day and night, watching the
hole. He'll come out in the end. He'll have to.

[*Bring out camp stools and bags of food from diggers. Sit, shotguns trained. Take supper out of bags.* BOGGIS: *boiled chicken.* BUNCE: *paper-bag containing doughnuts. And* BEAN: *flagon of cider*]

BOGGIS [*Waving chicken in front of him towards tunnel*]: Can you smell this, Mr Fox? Lovely tender chicken! Why don't you come up and get it?
[*Sound effect of* FOXES' *voices echoing as in tunnel.* FARMERS, *unaware of* FOXES' *voices, eat and drink, disgustingly and greedily*]

SMALL FOX 2: Oh Dad, just smell that smell! Couldn't we just sneak up and snatch it out of his hand?

MRS FOX: Don't you dare! That's just what they want you to do.

SMALL FOX 1: But we're so *hungry*!

SMALL FOX 3: How long will it be till we get something to eat?
[*Silence from tunnel*]

BEAN [*Unaware of* FOXES' *voices*]: Now we'll take it in turns to keep watch. One watches while two sleep, and so on through the night.

BOGGIS: What if the fox digs a hole right through the hill and comes out on the other side? You didn't think of that one, did you?

BEAN [*Pretending he had*]: Er, of course I did!

BOGGIS: Go on, then, tell us the answer.

BEAN [*Picking something small and black out of his ear and flicking it away*]: How many men have you got working on your farm?

BOGGIS: Thirty-five.

BUNCE: I've got thirty-six.

BEAN: And I've got thirty-seven. That makes one hundred and eight men altogether. We'll send word for them to surround the hill. Each man will have a gun and a flashlight. There will be no escape then for Mr Fox.

BOGGIS: We'll catch that blighter!

BUNCE: We've got him this time!

BEAN: Simply a matter of time.
[*Blackout. Sound recording*]

MR FOX: They're still there.

MRS FOX: Are you quite sure?

MR FOX: Positive. I can smell that man Bean a mile away. He *stinks*!
[*Silence*]

End of Scene 4

SCENE 5

Action takes place on stage in front of closed curtains. FOXES *are in the tunnel, weary and hungry.* MR FOX *sits, eyes closed, thoughtful.*

SMALL FOX 1: If only we could have just a tiny sip of water. Oh, Dad, can't you do something?

SMALL FOX 2: Three long days and three long nights we've been here. How long can we last out?

SMALL FOX 3: I keep dreaming about chickens, luscious and plump . . . and then I wake up.

SMALL FOX 4: Couldn't we make a dash for it, Dad? We'd have a little bit of a chance, wouldn't we?

MRS FOX: No chance at all. I refuse to let you go out there and face those guns. I'd sooner you stayed here and died in peace.

[*Silence, then* MR FOX *slowly rises to his feet. Spark of excitement in his eyes*]

MRS FOX: What is it, darling?

MR FOX [*Carefully*]: I've just had a bit of an idea.

SMALL FOXES: What? Oh, Dad, what is it?

MRS FOX: Come *on*! Tell us quickly!

MR FOX: Well ... [*Sits down again, sighing and shaking head sadly*] No, it's no good. It won't work after all.

SMALL FOX 4: Why not, Dad?

MR FOX: Because it means more digging and we aren't any of us strong enough for that after three days and nights without food.

SMALL FOX 1 [*Reviving*]: Yes we are, Dad!

SMALL FOX 2: Look at my muscles, Dad!

SMALL FOX 3: We can do it! You see if we can't! So can you!

SMALL FOX 4: Try and stop me, Dad!

MR FOX: I ... I suppose we could give it a try.

SMALL FOXES: Let's go, Dad! Tell us what you want us to do!

MRS FOX [*Getting up weakly*]: I am so sorry, but I don't think I am going to be much help.

MR FOX: You stay right where you are, my darling. We can handle this by ourselves. [SMALL FOXES *gather round* MR FOX] This time we must go in a very special direction.

SMALL FOX 1: Dad, I wish you would tell us *where* we're going.

SMALL FOX 2: Just one clue, Dad.

SMALL FOX 3: A tiny, tiny clue, Dad.

MR FOX: I dare not do that, because this place I am hoping to get to is so *marvellous* that if I described it to you now you would go crazy with excitement. And then if we failed to get there (which is very possible) you would die of disappointment. I don't want to raise your hopes too much, my darlings. Right [*Sniffs air and points to stage right*], we'll make off in this direction. I'll go first. Whiskers down and . . . DIG.

> [MR FOX *and* SMALL FOXES *begin digging. Digging music!* MRS FOX *slips through curtain.* FOXES *dig down ramp right and across auditorium floor to bottom of centre steps* (*Position A*). MR FOX *stops and sniffs*]

MR FOX: I think we had better take a peep upstairs now and see where we are. I know where I WANT to be, but I can't possibly be sure we're anywhere near it. [*Moves up to top step. Feels imaginary plank above his head*] It's wood. Wooden planks!

SMALL FOX 1: What does that mean, Dad?

MR FOX [*Whispering*]: It means, unless I am very much mistaken, that we are right underneath somebody's house. Be very quiet now while I take a peek. [*Slowly lifts up imaginary floorboards and puts his head through gap. As he does so, curtains pull back to reveal inside* BOGGIS's *Chicken House Number One*] I've done it! [*Shrieking*] I've done it, *first time*! I've done it! I've done it! Come on up! Come on up and see where you are, my darlings. What a sight for a hungry fox! Hallelujah! Hooray! Hooray!

[SMALL FOXES *scramble up on to stage. Rush round wild with excitement*]

SMALL FOX 4: Hundreds and hundreds of chickens – all for us. We need never starve now.

SMALL FOX 2: White ones [*Pointing*] . . . brown ones, black ones, spotty ones, big ones, littler ones, fat ones . . . [*Trails off*]

SMALL FOX 3 [*Continuing*]: Grey ones, red ones, dumpy ones, fluffy ones, giant ones . . .

SMALL FOX 1: If only old Boggis knew, he'd turn purple with rage.

SMALL FOX 4: I've never seen so many chickens before in my life!

SMALL FOX 2: It's like a dream. I have to keep pinching myself. What a plan, what a marvellous plan it was!

MR FOX [*To himself*]: Boggis's Chicken House Number One! It's exactly what I was aiming at! I hit it slap in the middle! First time! Isn't that fantastic! *And*, if I may say so, rather clever! Wait! [*To* SMALL FOXES *who are running around in all directions, chasing imaginary chickens*] Don't lose your heads! Stand back! Calm down! Let's do this properly! First of all, everyone have a drink of water!

SMALL FOX 1 [*After drinking from trough*]: Look at them, all perched up there. They look so stupid.

SMALL FOX 3 [*Wiping mouth*]: So would you if you had to live in here with that smell all day. I bet Boggis never ever cleans it out.

[MR FOX *drinks*]

SMALL FOX 2 [*Who is examining each corner of the Chicken House*]: I wonder where he expects them to lay their eggs. Perhaps that's what makes the awful smell – lots and lots of rotten eggs.

SMALL FOX 4 [*Chuckling*]: I bet they won't be laying any tonight after we've been here.

SMALL FOX 2: I wish Mum could be here to see all this. It's a foxes' paradise.

SMALL FOX 1: Yes. Never mind. We can tell her all about it. Dad, how can we carry all these back to Mum?

SMALL FOX 4: Shall we catch as many as we can?

MR FOX: Certainly not! We'll take three. [*Takes three chickens off their perch and holds them up*] We must be prudent. Right, now we'll go back to the tunnel. No fooling around, the quicker you move, the quicker you shall have something to eat. [*To* SMALL FOX 1] When we are in the tunnel, my son, you run back with these to your mother. Tell her to prepare a feast. Tell her the rest of us will be along in a jiffy, as soon as we have made a few other little arrangements. Now for the next bit, my darlings. [*Turns to others*] This one'll be as easy as pie! All we have to do is dig another little tunnel from *here* to there.

SMALL FOX 4: To where, Dad?

MR FOX: Don't ask so many questions. Start digging!

End of Scene 5

SCENE 6

Action takes place in front of curtain. Darkness. FOXES *enter stage left, digging across stage. Spotlight on* FOXES. *One small* FOX *holds a light.*

MR FOX: Keep digging. It's not much further.

MR BADGER [*Loud voice from behind curtain*]: Who goes there?

> [FOXES *jump and stop;* MR FOX *peers through gloom.* MR BADGER *and* SMALL BADGER *appear through slit in curtain with light in hand. Lights go up*]

MR FOX: Badger!

MR BADGER: Foxy! My goodness me, I'm glad I've found *someone* at last! I've been digging around in circles for three days and nights and I haven't the foggiest idea where I am. [MR FOX *and* MR BADGER *shake hands.* SMALL FOXES *and* SMALL BADGER *exchange friendly punches*] Haven't you *heard* what's happening up on the hill? It's chaos. Half the wood has disappeared and there are men with guns all over the countryside. None of us can get out, even at night. We're all starving to death.

MR FOX: Who is *we*?

MR BADGER: All us diggers. That's me and Mole, and

Rabbit, and all our wives and children. Even Weasel, who can usually sneak out of the tightest spots, is right now hiding down my hole with Mrs Weasel ánd six kids. What on earth are we going to do, Foxy? I think we're finished.

MR FOX [*Smiling secretly at three* SMALL FOXES]: My dear old Badger, this mess you're in is all my fault . . .

MR BADGER [*Furious*]: I *know* it's your fault. And the farmers are not going to give up till they've got you. Unfortunately, that means *us* as well. It means everyone on the hill. We're done for. [*Puts arm round* SMALL BADGER] My poor wife back there is so weak she can't dig another yard.

MR FOX: Nor can mine. And yet [*Enjoying the sensationalism of the part*], at this very minute she is preparing for me and my children the most delicious feast of plump juicy chickens.

MR BADGER: Stop! Don't tease me! I can't stand it!

SMALL FOX 2: It's true! Dad's not teasing! We've got chickens galore!

MR FOX: And because everything is entirely my fault, I invite you to share the feast. I invite *everyone* to share it – you and Mole and Rabbit and Weasel and all your wives and children. There'll be plenty to go round, I can assure you.

MR BADGER: You mean it? You *really mean* it?

MR FOX [*Conspiratorially to* MR BADGER]: Do you know where we've just been?

MR BADGER: Where?

MR FOX: Right inside Boggis's Chicken House Number One!

MR BADGER *and* SMALL BADGER: No!

MR FOX: Yes! But that is nothing to where we are going now. You have come just at the right moment, my dear Badger. You can help us dig. And in the meanwhile your small son can run back to Mrs Badger and all the others and spread the good news. [*To* SMALL BADGER] Tell them they are invited to a Fox's Feast. Then bring them all down here and follow this tunnel back until you find my home.

SMALL BADGER: Yes, Mr Fox! Yes, sir! Right away, sir! Oh, thank you sir!
    [*Exit stage left*]

MR FOX: We go this way, Badger, old chap.
    [*Turns and points to stage right, with back to Badger*]

MR BADGER: My dear Foxy! What in the world has happened to your tail?

MR FOX: Don't talk about it *please*. It's a painful subject. Nose down, and DIG. [*Digging music. Dig along stage towards stage right, down ramp along auditorium floor to Position A as before.* MR FOX *climbs up steps. Feels imaginary floorboards above head as before*] If I am not mistaken, my dear Badger [*Whispering*], we are now underneath the farm which belongs to that nasty little pot-bellied dwarf, Bunce. We are, in fact, directly underneath the most INTERESTING *part* of that farm.

SMALL FOXES: Ducks and geese. Juicy tender ducks and big fat geese.

MR FOX: Ex-*actly*.

MR BADGER: But how in the world can you know where we are?

MR FOX [*Grinning*]: Look, I know my way around these farms, blindfold. For me it's just as easy below ground as it is above it. [*Puts his head through imaginary floorboard. Curtains open to reveal inside of* BUNCE'S *Mighty Storehouse, packed full of ducks and geese*] Yes, I've done it again! [*Jumping on to stage, others follow, gape in wonder*] I've hit it smack on the nose. Right in the bull's-eye. Come and look! [MR BADGER *and three* SMALL FOXES *scramble up steps*] This, my dear old Badger, is Bunce's Mighty Storehouse! All his finest stuff is stored here before he sends it off to market. Just feast your eyes on *that*. What do you think of it, eh? Pretty good grub. [MR BADGER *and* SMALL ONES *run forward to grab at food*] Stop! This is *my* party, so *I* shall do the choosing. We mustn't overdo it. Mustn't give the game away! Mustn't let them know what we've been up to. We must be neat and tidy and take just a few of the choicest morsels. So, to start with we shall have four plump young ducks! [*Reaches up for four from shelf*] Oh, how lovely and fat they are. No wonder Bunce gets a special price for them in the market. All right, Badger, lend me a hand to get them down. You children can help as well ... There we go ... Goodness me, look how your mouths are watering ... And now ... I think we had better have a few geese ... [MR BADGER *and* SMALL FOXES *help* MR FOX *as he talks*] There will be quite enough ... we'll take the biggest ... Oh my, oh my, you'll never see finer geese than these in a king's kitchen ... Gently does it ... that's the way ... And what about a couple of nice smoked hams ... I adore smoked ham, don't you, Badger?

MR BADGER: I'm mad about bacon. [*Dancing with excitement*] Let's have a side of bacon. The big one up there!

SMALL FOX 2: And carrots, Dad. We must take some of those carrots.

MR FOX: Don't be a twerp. You know we never eat things like that.

SMALL FOX 2: It's not for us, Dad. It's for the Rabbits. They only eat vegetables.

MR FOX: My goodness me, you're right. What a thoughtful little fellow you are. Take ten bunches of carrots.

SMALL FOX 3: And there's some turnips over there.

SMALL FOX 4: And I'll get those lettuces.

MR FOX: And now, we shall have to borrow from our friend Bunce one of those useful push-carts over in the corner. Can you load it up children, please.
[MR BADGER *pauses suddenly and takes* MR FOX *to one side*]

MR BADGER: Doesn't this worry you just a tiny bit, Foxy?

MR FOX: Worry me? What?

MR BADGER: All this . . . this stealing.

MR FOX [*Arm around* MR BADGER]: My dear old furry frump, do you know anyone in the *whole world* who wouldn't swipe a few chickens if his children were starving to death? [*Pause as* MR BADGER *thinks*] You are far too respectable.

MR BADGER: There's nothing wrong with being respectable.

MR FOX: Look, Boggis and Bunce and Bean are out to *kill us.* You realize that, I hope?

MR BADGER: I do, Foxy, I do indeed.

MR FOX: But we're not going to stoop to *their* level. We don't want to kill *them.*

MR BADGER: I should hope not, indeed.

MR FOX: We wouldn't dream of it. We shall simply take a little food here and there to keep us and our families alive. Right?

MR BADGER: I suppose we'll have to.

MR FOX: If *they* want to be horrible, let them. We down here are decent, peace-loving people.

MR BADGER [*Gently*]: Foxy, I love you.

MR FOX: Thank you. Now, my darlings [*To* SMALL FOX 2 *and* SMALL FOX 3], take the cart and run back as fast as you can to your mother. Give her my love, and tell her we are having guests for dinner – the Badgers, the Moles, the Rabbits and the Weasels. Tell her the rest of us will be home as soon as we've done one more little job.

SMALL FOXES 2 *and* 3 [*Still filling up carts*]: Yes, Dad. Right away, Dad. We've nearly finished.

MR FOX: And now, just one more visit.

SMALL FOX 4: And I'll bet I know where that'll be.

MR BADGER: Where?

SMALL FOX 4: Well, we've been to Boggis and we've been to Bunce, but we haven't been to Bean. It must be Bean.

MR FOX: You're right. But what you don't know

is which *part* of Bean's place we are about to visit.

MR BADGER: Well, tell us – which?

MR FOX: Ah-ha. Just you wait and see.

End of Scene 6

SCENE 7

Curtains open. No lights. Spotlight on MR FOX, SMALL FOX 4 *and* MR BADGER *as they enter stage right. Approach small wall of cardboard boxes, about six feet from stage right wings.*

MR BADGER: What on earth is this? It looks like a solid stone wall. [*Animals scrape away in front of it*] Now who in the world would build a wall under the ground?

MR FOX: Very simple. It's the wall of an underground room. And if I am not mistaken, it is exactly what I'm looking for.
> [MR FOX *continues to investigate the wall. He pulls away a loose 'brick'. Lights go up to show* BEAN'S *dark and gloomy cellar.* RAT *is on the other side of the wall, looking through hole to* MR FOX]

RAT: Go away! You can't come in here! It's private!

MR BADGER: Good Lord! It's Rat!

MR FOX: You saucy beast! I should have guessed we'd find you down here somewhere.

RAT [*Shrieking*]: Go away! Go on, beat it! This is my private pitch!

MR FOX: Shut up.

RAT: I will not shut up! This is *my* place! I got here first!

MR FOX [*Softly*]: My dear Rat, I am a hungry fellow, and if you don't hop it quickly, I shall eat-you-up-in-one-gulp.
[RAT *scurries to other side of stage.* MR FOX *laughs and pulls out more 'bricks'. He crawls through.* BADGER *and* SMALL FOX 4 *follow*]

MR FOX: This is it!

MR BADGER: This is *what*? The place is empty.

SMALL FOX 4: Where are the turkeys? I thought Bean was a turkey man.

MR FOX: He is a turkey man. But we're not after turkeys now. We've got plenty of food.

SMALL FOX 4: Then what *do* we need, Dad?

MR FOX: Take a good look round. Don't you see *anything* that interests you?
[MR BADGER *and* SMALL FOX *peer round shelves, eventually finding several flagons, ranging from very large to small sizes, labelled* 'CIDER']

SMALL FOX 4: Oh, Dad! Look what we've found! It's cider!

MR FOX: Ex-*actly*!

MR BADGER [*Shouting*]: Tremendous!

MR FOX: Bean's Secret Cider Cellar. But go carefully, my dears. Don't make a noise. This cellar is right underneath the farmhouse itself.

MR BADGER: Cider is especially good for Badgers. We take it as medicine – one large glass three times a day with meals and another at bedtime.

MR FOX: It will make the feast into a banquet.

SMALL FOX 4 [*Removes a small jar off a shelf and takes a gulp*]: Wow! Wowee! Ah – h – h – h. This is *some cider!*

MR FOX: That's quite enough of that. [*Grabs jar and puts it to his own lips*] It's miraculous! It's fabulous! It's beautiful!

MR BADGER: It's my turn. [*Takes gulp*] It's . . . it's like melted gold! Oh Foxy, it's . . . like drinking sunbeams and rainbows!
      [RAT *is lying indolently in front of several large flagons standing on the floor, sucking cider through a tube going through the neck of one of the flagons*]

RAT: You're poaching! Put that down at once! There'll be none left for me!

MR FOX: You're drunk!

RAT: Mind your own business! And if you great clumsy brutes come messing about in here, we'll all be caught. Get out and leave me to sip my cider in peace.

MRS BEAN [*Off-stage*]: Hurry up and get that cider, Mabel! You know Mr Bean doesn't like to be kept waiting, especially when he's been out all night in the cold.

> [*Sound of a door opening and footsteps coming down to the cellar*]

MR FOX: Quick! Hide!

> [*All three plus RAT hide behind the row of large flagons. MABEL enters stage left and starts looking slowly and deliberately along the shelves of cider jars. She carries a rolling pin*]

MABEL [*Shouting to MRS BEAN*]: How many will he want this time, Mrs Bean?

MRS BEAN [*Off-stage*]: Bring up two or three jars.

MABEL: He drank four yesterday, Mrs Bean.

MRS BEAN [*Off-stage*]: Yes, but he won't want that many today because he's not going to be up there more than a few hours longer. He says the fox is bound to make a run for it, this morning. It can't possibly stay down that hole another day without food.

MABEL [*Removing jar from shelf close to MR FOX's head*]: I'll be glad when the rotten brute is killed and strung up on the front porch. And by the way, Mrs Bean, your husband promised I could have the tail as a souvenir.

MRS BEAN [*Off-stage*]: The tail's been all shot to pieces. Didn't you know that?

MABEL: You mean it's *ruined*?

MRS BEAN [*Off-stage*]: Of course it's ruined. They shot the tail but missed the fox.

MABEL: Oh heck! I did so want the tail!

MRS BEAN [*Off-stage*]: You can have the head instead, Mabel. You can get it stuffed and hang it on your bedroom wall. Hurry up now with that cider!

MABEL: Yes, ma'am, I'm coming. [*Removes a second jar off shelf. If next jar is taken,* MR FOX*'s head will be seen*] Will two be enough, Mrs Bean, or shall I take three?

MRS BEAN [*Off stage*]: My goodness, Mabel, I don't care so long as you get a move on.

MABEL: Then two it is. [*To herself*] He drinks too much anyway. [*Jar in each hand, rolling pin tucked under one arm, she goes to door stage left, pauses and sniffs*] There's rats down here again, Mrs Bean, I can smell 'em.

MRS BEAN [*Off-stage*]: Then poison them, woman, poison them! You know where the poison's kept.

MABEL: Yes, Ma'am. [*Exits stage left. Her footsteps are heard climbing slowly upstairs. Door slams*]

MR FOX [*Coming out, with others from behind flagons*]: Quick! Grab a jar each and run for it!

RAT [*Shrieking and dancing about*]: What did I tell you! You nearly got nabbed, didn't you? You nearly gave the game away! You keep out of here from now on! I don't want you around! This is my place!

MR FOX: You . . . [*Poking him in the chest*] . . . are going to be poisoned.

RAT: Poppycock! I sit up here and *watch* her putting the stuff down. She'll never get *me*.

MR FOX, MR BADGER *and* SMALL FOX 4 [*Climbing back through the hole in the wall, each clutching a jar*]: Goodbye, Rat. Thanks for the lovely cider!

RAT [*Jumping about in rage*]: Thieves! Robbers! Bandits! Burglars!
     [*Lights fade. Spotlight on* MR FOX *and* SMALL FOX 4, *on other side of wall.* MR FOX *is putting 'bricks' back*]

MR FOX: I can still taste that glorious cider. What an impudent fellow Rat is.

MR BADGER: He has bad manners. All rats have bad manners. I've never met a polite rat yet.

MR FOX: And he drinks too much. [*Putting last 'brick' in place*] There we are. Now home to the feast.

End of Scene 7

SCENE 8

BOGGIS, BUNCE *and* BEAN *take up waiting positions at B, sitting on camp stools, slumped over guns on laps. Curtain opens. Huge table with animals around it. Everyone eating and talking.* MRS FOX *and* MRS BADGER *are going round filling up plates. Air of great festivity.*

MRS FOX: Eat up, everybody! Thanks to my wonderful, marvellous husband, there's enough for two or even three helpings. You must all be so hungry!

MR MOLE: It was becoming a nightmare. Every time I popped my head above ground, I found myself staring down the barrel of a gun.

MRS MOLE: We were so worried for the children. It's so difficult to keep an eye on them all the time.

MR WEASEL: We had the same problem. Very tricky. Tried everything. Crafty little things. Always giving me the slip. [*To* MRS WEASEL] Didn't they, dear? I'll have another chicken leg, while you're passing, Mrs Fox, if you don't mind.

MRS WEASEL: You're right. But we were all getting so hungry, that was the chief worry. And now we're sitting down in front of this wonderful feast! Your husband deserves a medal, Mrs Fox. Oh my, is that really smoked ham?

MRS RABBIT: You know it was so thoughtful of your husband, Mrs Fox, to send back those carrots and lettuces. I've never tasted fresher ones.

MRS BADGER [*Calls across table*]: How are you doing with that dish, Mrs Fox? Shall I bring in reinforcements?

MRS FOX: I think we're all right, dear.

MR RABBIT [*Mouth full*]: This is wonderful, truly wonderful! We should have all got together before.

MRS MOLE: This duck is delicious! I really must have the recipe from you, Mrs Fox. And there's so much!

MRS FOX: Well, Mrs Badger shared the cooking and of course the children helped.

MRS WEASEL: If you young ones have had enough, you can get down.

SMALL WEASEL: Listen to this, Mum!
[*At one table* SMALL FOX 2 *starts to sing*]

> Oh Boggis and Bunce and Bean,
> One fat, one short, one lean,
> Those horrible crooks,
> So different in looks,
> Were none the less equally mean.

[*Laughter*]

SMALL RABBIT: Badger's made up another verse. Shhh!

[SMALL BADGER *climbs on table. Silence as he sings*]

Oh Boggis and Bunce and Bean,
One fat, one short, one lean,
Faces crack when they smile,
You can smell 'em a mile,
We all scarper as soon as they're seen.
[*Laughter*]

MRS FOX: Shh, everybody, I can hear something from
the tunnel.
[*Assembly slowly settles. From outside the door they
hear* MR FOX *singing in a rich tenor voice*]

MR FOX: Home again swiftly I glide,
Back to my beautiful bride,
She'll not feel so rotten
As soon as she's gotten
Some cider inside her inside.
[*Then*]

MR BADGER: Oh poor Mrs Badger, he cried,
So hungry she very near died,
But she'll not feel so hollow
If only she'll swallow
Some cider inside her inside.
[MRS FOX *and* MRS BADGER *visibly melt.* MR FOX,
MR BADGER *and* SMALL FOX 4 *burst in*]

MRS FOX: My darling! [*Hugging* MR FOX] We couldn't
wait! Please forgive us.
[*Everyone hugs* MR FOX, MR BADGER *and* SMALL

FOX 4. *There is much hilarity and back-slapping.*
All sit down and continue eating. Shouts of 'Pass Dad
the duck', 'More cider for Mr Badger', 'Tell us all
about it', etc. The three eat ravenously, then contentedly
pause and lean back]

MR BADGER [*Stands, raising his mug*]: A toast! I want
you all to stand and drink a toast to our dear friend
who has saved our lives this day – Mr Fox!

ALL: To Mr Fox! [*All stand and raise glasses*] To Mr Fox!
Long may he live!

MRS FOX [*Shyly*]: I don't want to make a speech. I just
want to say one thing and it is this: MY HUS-
BAND IS A FANTASTIC FOX.
[*All clap and cheer*]

MR FOX [*Standing*]: This delicious meal . . . [*He belches*
. . . laughter and applause] This delicious meal, my
friends, is by courtesy of Messrs Boggis, Bunce and
Bean. [*More cheering and laughter*] And I hope you
have enjoyed it as much as I have.
[*Belches again*]

MR BADGER: Better out than in.

MR FOX [*Grinning*]: Thank you. But now, my friends,
let us be serious. Let us think of tomorrow, and the
next day and the days after that. If we go out, we will
be killed. Right?

ALL: Right!

MR BADGER: We'll be shot before we've gone a yard.

MR FOX: Ex-*actly*. But who *wants* to go out, anyway; let me ask you that? We are all diggers, every one of us. We hate the outside. The outside is full of enemies. We only go out because we have to, to get food for our families. But now, my friends, we have an entirely new set-up. We have a safe tunnel leading to three of the finest stores in the world!

MR BADGER: We do indeed! I've seen 'em.

MR FOX: And you know what this means? *It means that none of us need ever go out into the open again!* [*Muttering of assembled company*] I therefore invite you all to stay here with me for ever.

ALL: For ever! My goodness! How marvellous!

MR RABBIT [*To* MRS RABBIT]: My dear, just think! We're never going to be shot at again in our lives!

MR FOX: We will make a little underground village, with streets and houses on each side – separate houses for the Badgers and Moles and Rabbits and Weasels and Foxes. And every day I will go shopping for you all. And every day [*Rising to a crescendo*] we will eat like kings.

> [*Cheering and shouting. Curtains close slowly. Spotlight turns to* BOGGIS, BUNCE *and* BEAN. *Sound of rainwater*]

BOGGIS: He won't stay down there much longer now!

BUNCE: The brute must be famished.

BEAN: That's right. He'll be making a dash for it any moment. Keep your guns handy.

[*Lights fade. Sound of rainwater becomes louder*]

Curtain

LIGHTING CUES

SCENE 1

1. CHILDREN's entrance. *Spotlight*
2. FIRST CHILD: 'I think old Boggis is the worst . . .' *Second spotlight* on BOGGIS
3. SECOND CHILD: '. . . pot-bellied dwarf Bunce then?' *Second spotlight moves to* BUNCE
4. THIRD CHILD: '. . . revolting than old Bean.' *Second spotlight moves to* BEAN
5. CHILDREN: 'Stop! Ugh!' *Single spotlight* on CHILDREN until exit
6. CHILDREN's exit. *Full lights* on BOGGIS, BUNCE and BEAN

SCENE 2

1. *Lights only* on part of stage which is inside of FOXES' hole
2. MR FOX: '. . . I'll see you later.' *Lights out* on FOXES' hole. *Spotlight on* MR FOX
3. BANG, BANG, BANG. *Lights off. Spotlight* on BOGGIS, BUNCE and BEAN appearing behind trees

SCENE 3

1. *Lights only* on inside FOXES' hole
2. MRS FOX: 'Good-night.' *Lights out*

3. MR FOX: 'Ouch!' Silence. *Dim lights* on BOGGIS, BUNCE and BEAN entering stage left

4. MR FOX: 'Wake up!' *Lights* on FOXES' hole

5. MR FOX: '. . . Come on. DIG.' *Spotlight follows* FOXES down ramp

SCENE 4

1. Entrance of mechanical shovels. *Lights* on stage. *Spotlight* on FOXES at bottom of ramp

2. *Spotlights follow* BOGGIS, BUNCE, BEAN and FOXES as they move through auditorium. As BOGGIS, BUNCE and BEAN reach bottom of ramp, *lights go out* on stage

SCENE 5

1. *Dim lighting* on stage at opening of scene (tunnel)

2. *Stage lighting off* as FOXES reach bottom of ramp. *Spotlight follows* them across auditorium floor

3. MR FOX: '. . . while I take a peek.' *Momentary blackout*

4. Curtains open. *Full stage lights*

SCENE 6

1. *Spotlight* on FOXES who enter stage left. *Dim stage lighting*

2. MR BADGER enters through curtain. *Lights go up*

3. *Stage lights off* as FOXES and MR BADGER reach bottom of ramp. *Spotlight follows* them across auditorium floor

4. MR FOX: '. . . as it is above it.' *Momentary blackout* – curtains open – *full stage lights*

SCENE 7

1. *Spotlight on* FOXES and MR BADGER entering stage right

2. MR FOX pulls away first loose brick. *Dim light* on Bean's Secret Cider Cellar, stage right of 'wall'

3. As FOXES and MR BADGER climb through wall, *stage lights* on Bean's Secret Cider Cellar

4. 'Goodbye, Rat.' *Lights fade* as FOXES and MR BADGER climb back through 'wall'

5. MR FOX: 'And he drinks too much.' Puts last brick back in place. *Lights out* on Bean's Secret Cider Cellar. *Spotlight follows* FOXES and MR BADGER off stage left

SCENE 8

1. *Full lights* as curtains open

2. '. . . We will eat like kings.' Curtains close – *blackout*

3. *Spotlight* on BOGGIS, BUNCE and BEAN at Position B

4. BEAN: 'Keep your guns handy.' *Spotlight fades*

SOUND CUES

SCENE 2

1. MR FOX climbs up steps outside den. Edges out to waist. Sniffs. *Rustle*
2. MR FOX ... long, careful look round. *Bang, bang, bang* (gunshots)

SCENE 3

1. BOGGIS, BUNCE and BEAN enter stage left and begin *shovelling* noisily outside FOXES' door (optional; sufficient noise could be made by FARMERS on stage)
2. MRS FOX: '. . . outwit those awful men.' *Loud scrunch* (splitting door)
3. MRS FOX: '. . . Your father is a fantastic fox.' *Crash* (door breaks down)

SCENE 4

1. Scene opens. Sound of approaching *mechanical shovels*. This sound accompanies FARMERS as they dig. Stops during periods of dialogue.
2. MR FOX: 'Dig! Dig! Dig!' *Digging music*. While music is playing, *digger* sound lowered.
3. MRS FOX: '. . . We must shake them off soon, surely.' *Loud crunching sound*
4. BOGGIS: '. . . Why don't you come up and get it?'

Sound recording of FOXES' voices (echoing as in tunnel)

5. Blackout at end of scene. *Sound recording* of FOXES' voices

SCENE 5

1. MR FOX: '...Whiskers down and ... DIG.' *Digging music* until MR FOX stops and sniffs

2. Curtains open to reveal inside of BOGGIS's Chicken House Number 1. *Clucking* and *squawking* (optional)

SCENE 6

1. MR FOX: '... Nose down, and DIG.' *Digging music* until MR FOX stops at Position A

SCENE 7

1. MRS BEAN [*Off-stage*] '... when he's been out all night in the cold.' *Door opening, footsteps climbing down to cellar*

2. MABEL: 'Yes, ma'am.' *Footsteps climbing slowly upstairs. Door slams*

SCENE 8

1. Curtains close. Spotlight on BOGGIS, BUNCE and BEAN at Position B. *Rainwater*

2. BEAN: '... Keep your guns handy.' Lights fade. *Rainwater becomes louder*

DIGGING MUSIC

It is important that 'digging music' should be pleasing to the audience, that they should not tire of it, and, even better, that they should go away humming it. The extent to which the music is played during the periods of the Chase and subsequent digging is up to the producer. However, there are some wonderful opportunities for mime during these times, both by the Foxes and the Farmers, and this can be developed to fit in with the music chosen. In some of the pieces there are natural climaxes that can coincide with periods of frantic digging and subsequent dialogue. Two suggestions for suitable music are the 'Tritsch-Tratsch' polka by Johann Strauss II and the Russian Dance from Tchaikovsky's *The Nutcracker*. Or why not compose your own?

There are, of course, many opportunities to introduce music at other points in the play, especially in the final scene.

SCENERY AND PROPERTIES

Most items of scenery, such as trees, chicken perches, large bricks, can be made fairly simply out of cardboard, either corrugated or from large boxes, and if necessary supported by wooden framework. The wall separating Bean's Secret Cider Cellar from the tunnel need only be several cardboard boxes, painted to look like large bricks and taped together for strength. It stands at right angles to the edge of the stage, and Mr Fox has only to remove the one loose brick to climb through the wall.

Most props, such as shotguns, chickens (boiled or otherwise) and shovels, may likewise be made out of cardboard, papier mâché or other materials readily accessible in schools, and liberally coated with paint or feathers. A handcart may be an orange box fixed on to a pair of old pram wheels. Masks are always a problem, as there is the danger of hiding actors' faces or expressions. If used, they should sit on the top of the head and not over the face. The only major items that may present some difficulties are the mechanical diggers.

MECHANICAL DIGGERS
Make two cardboard cutouts of the lower part and tracks of the diggers, attached to a lightweight timber framework, and joined laterally by strengthening bars.

Mechanical digger

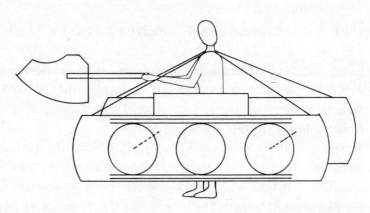

Attach straps or strips of material from two points of each cutout to rest over the actors' shoulders and to lift the digger at least a few inches off the ground. Attach two pieces of wood to the outside of a box, suitably shovel-shaped, and to be held by the actor and 'worked' accordingly. If there is a problem carrying camp stools and bags during this scene, either Boggis can be assigned to carry the luggage, or these can be placed at Position B during the previous blackout.

LIST OF PROPERTIES

Scene 1
Food: boiled chickens, doughnuts, flagons of cider
Plates, some cutlery

Scene 2
Ironing board, iron, clothes to iron
Board game and dice
Scarf
Torch
Flask·
Three shotguns

Scene 3
Bowl, scissors, bandages
Torches
Shovels
Flask

Scene 4
Two diggers
Bags containing boiled chickens, doughnuts, flask
Camp stools
Watch (BOGGIS)

Scene 5
Three chickens (picked up by MR FOX)

Scene 6
Light (SMALL FOX)
Light (MR BADGER)
Four plump ducks
Four geese
Two hams
Ten bunches carrots
Turnips
Lettuces
Pushcart

Scene 7
Flagons of cider
Tube (RAT)
Rolling pin

Scene 8
Food: chickens, ducks, lettuces, etc.
Plates, mugs, cutlery
Shotguns (BOGGIS, BUNCE and BEAN)
Camp stools

SUGGESTIONS FOR STAGING AND SET

Ideas for staging and set would seem to be best left to the imagination of the producer and stage manager. At St Andrew's School, staff, governors, parents and children are all involved in producing backdrops, scenery, properties and costumes. Each group or school will have its own ideas. The scene that poses the most problems, set-wise, is Scene 2, which incorporates both the inside and the outside of the Foxes' hole.

SET FOR SCENE 2

(See Staging Plan on p. 76)

Two-thirds of the stage is taken up by the Foxes' hole, with the door, not quite at right angles to the front of the stage, and left of centre stage. Outside the door are steps leading to a raised area on which stands a tree. Behind this lurk Boggis, Bunce and Bean. The raised part of the stage may be supported by forms or boxes. The tree can be made of cardboard, supported by pieces of wood.

The Foxes' hole consists of three hinged flats and contains, among other things, a bed, an ironing board and a mat. To confirm that the wind is blowing *away* from the farmers, a weather vane may be attached to the end of the stage left flat!

The door is freestanding and hinged inside a wooden

frame which is supported by two triangles of wood also hinged to the frame. At the blackout at the end of Scene 2 the supporting triangles on the door may be folded in, so that Boggis, Bunce and Bean may actually break down the door by pushing it over.

The whole set is two to three feet from the front of the stage, which enables Bunce and Bean to drive their mechanical shovels on from stage left, straight across the front of the stage and down the ramp stage right.

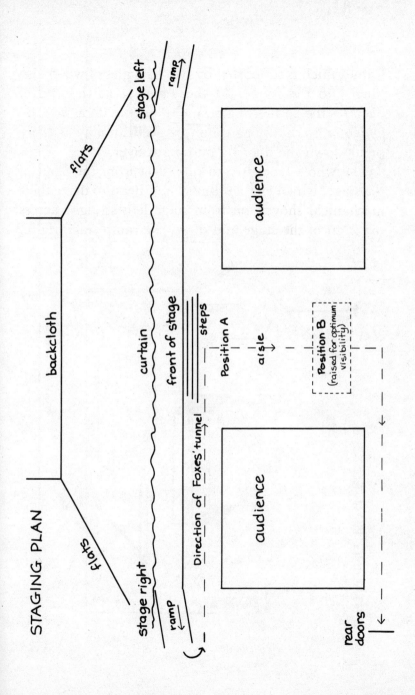

STAGING PLAN

flats

stage right

ramp

backcloth

flats

stage left

ramp

curtain

front of stage

Direction of Foxes' tunnel

steps

Position A

aisle

Position B
(raised for optimum visibility)

audience

audience

rear
doors

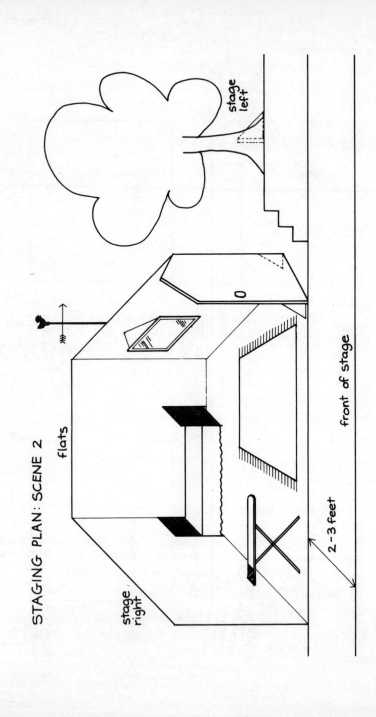

STAGING PLAN: SCENE 2

flats

stage right

stage left

front of stage

2 - 3 feet

WAGGLE YOUR EARS

Or, as the BFG would say, *swiggle* your ears and listen to your favourite Roald Dahl story in your room, in the car, on your way to school or the zoo or to buy chocolate . . .

Listen and laugh as **top-name actors**, including **Stephen Fry**, **Kate Winslet**, **David Walliams** and **Douglas Hodge**, bring your best-loved Roald Dahl moments to life.

Available on Puffin Audio

Scan the code for PHIZZ-WHIZZING audio clips!

THERE'S MORE TO ROALD DAHL THAN GREAT STORIES . . .

Did you know that 10% of Roald Dahl's royalties* from this book go to help the work of the Roald Dahl charities?

Roald Dahl is famous for his stories and rhymes, but much less well known is how often he went out of his way to help seriously ill children. Today **Roald Dahl's Marvellous Children's Charity** helps children with the severest conditions and the greatest needs. The charity believes every child can have a more marvellous life, no matter how ill they are, or how short their life may be.

Can you do something marvellous to help others? Find out how at **www.roalddahlcharity.org**

You can find out about Roald Dahl's real-life experiences and how they found their way into his stories at the **Roald Dahl Museum and Story Centre** in Great Missenden, Buckinghamshire (the author's home village). The Museum is a charity that aims to inspire excitement about reading, writing and creativity. There are three fun and fact-packed galleries, with lots to make, do and see (including Roald Dahl's writing hut). Aimed at 6–12-year-olds, the Museum is open to the public and to school groups throughout the year.

Find out more at **www.roalddahlmuseum.org**

Roald Dahl's Marvellous Children's Charity (RDMCC) is a registered charity no. 1137409.
The Roald Dahl Museum and Story Centre (RDMSC) is a registered charity no. 1085853.
The Roald Dahl Charitable Trust is a registered charity no. 1119330 and supports the work of RDMCC and RDMSC.

* Donated royalties are net of commission